STOLEN MAN

The Story of the Amistad Rebellion

I am indebted to the Amistad project of the Mystic Seaport Museum in Connecticut for the extensive research they have made available as well as to the University of Missouri-Kansas City School of Law, for their collection of primary documents and court records on the Amistad rebellion and trial.

I would also like to thank the many people who read the various drafts of my story over the years, offering me helpful suggestions and comments. I am particularly grateful for the insights and help of readers Nancy Heller, Carrie Jean Wharton, my wife Roni, my daughter Sierra and my cousin Susan who each brought a distinct view that guided this story along.

Typography and cover design by Chris Abshire
Cover photography: Michael G. Stewart and iStockphoto.com

⌁ ONE ~

Sengbe heard the sound of breaking branches and knew immediately he was in danger. It was not a sound that a bird or small animal would make but not loud enough for a lion, either. He crouched low toward the ground, even though he knew that whatever beast was in the forest had already spotted him and was not afraid.

Now there were more noises – human voices – coming from the other direction. These were angry voices shouting to each other in a language that Sengbe did not understand. They were certainly not speaking the Mende words he knew.

Sengbe turned and saw four men moving along the Mani road. They were yelling and pointing into the brush where he was squatting . These were not men he knew from any of the villages. They were strange people with skin darker than his.

Sengbe thought about the money he owed one of the villagers near his home. Could these men be after him because he had not paid the debt? He knew that sometimes men and women were taken away by warring tribes from other villages and sold or traded as slaves because of something they had done wrong. Was this why they were after him?

Sengbe also remembered the stories he had heard as a young boy about "devil men" who roamed the forest, grabbing people and taking them away. He had told these stories to his own children even though he doubted they were really true. He had always thought his mother and father told him these stories when he was a boy just to frighten him into staying close to the village. He repeated these stories to his own son and daughters for this reason.

Sengbe knew this forest well, and knew if he could get to the river, the noise of the water would disguise the sounds and help him escape. But the river was far away and now more men were running towards the spot where he was hiding. He knew he would be captured if he stayed where he was. There was only one way out so he began to run in the direction of the river, faster than he had ever run before.

But it was no use. As soon as he moved, the men were upon him. They wrestled him to the ground and began hitting him with sticks. The men pulled him up and tied his hands behind his back with a rope, shouting angry words that Sengbe could not understand.

᠃ TWO ᠂

Sengbe had been captured. His stomach hurt from where he had been beaten and the rope around his wrists now cut into his skin.

The men pushed and poked Sengbe with their sticks as they walked along the road together. They finally reached a clearing where other men from the villages surrounding Sengbe's home were gathered. Everyone was seated on the ground and Sengbe could see that many of these men had also been beaten. One man was bleeding from behind his ear and another man lay on the ground, coughing and spitting up blood. All of them had their hands tied behind their backs, just like Sengbe.

But it wasn't just the men who were gathered together. Sengbe could see that a few hundred feet away was another group from the villages. These were women and their hands were tied as well, although most had their hands bound in front of them.

With the women were a few children who were crying and screaming, but no one seemed to be paying any attention to them. The crying children reminded Sengbe of his own children.

Would he be able to hold his two daughters in his arms again? Would his son know what had happened to him? Would his wife go looking for him and get caught as well? Would he see his family again?

And who were these strange men that had taken him and what were they doing so close to his village? Sengbe had so many questions but no answers to any of them. He could hear his heart beating louder and louder in his chest. Or maybe it wasn't just his heart beating; maybe it was the hearts of all the men, women and children that were gathered together, beating louder and louder reminding him of the Mende drums of his people beating out a warning.

Sengbe closed his eyes hoping that this was a dream but when he opened them seconds later, everything was the same. This was not a bad dream. This was really happening.

☙ THREE ☙

Sengbe and the others were forced to sit in a circle with their hands tied behind their backs. After a while, one of the older men from a nearby village stood up and began talking to one of the captors and Sengbe could tell that neither could understand the words of the other. The strange dark man shouted at the older man and pushed him back down with his stick. He fell in the spot where the others were sitting. This caused everyone to begin shouting and talking all at once. One woman saw her chance and while the captured men were being quieted, she ran off into the forest. Sengbe wished he had fled instead of the woman, but there was no chance for that. His group was being watched too closely. Perhaps at night, Sengbe thought, when it was dark, he could sneak away unnoticed.

Before night came however, more strange men came and joined the first group. With these strange men were other men with white skin. These white-faced men smelled bad and carried guns and long poles that had openings at the end like the yokes you would use for animals. Sengbe's head was placed into one of the openings of the pole just like an ox. A rope was then tied around the opening so that he was unable to move his head in any direction. He could hear that someone else was being tied to the opening on the other end. With his hands still tied behind his back – and now with his head tied like an ox – Sengbe knew he had lost his chance to escape. He could see that everyone was being yoked together this way.

These devils were smart, Sengbe realized. They had thought of everything.

~ FOUR ~

The next morning, the men with guns got everyone up and they all began walking. Sengbe did not know where they were going, but they walked for many hours. As they walked, they were joined by other men and women who were also tied together, followed by more strange looking men with white faces and long guns.

Night came and they were allowed to sleep but with the next sun, they were being poked and shoved and forced to walk again.

Sengbe hurt all over. He had not eaten since he left his home and although he was allowed water, these men were clearly not going to feed him. Some of the prisoners fell as they marched along, but were forced to get up and walk more.

"How many suns have we been walking?" Sengbe wondered. He could not remember. After a few days, Sengbe could smell the smoke of a fire pit. Later that day they reached some sort of a camp and the strange men untied the ropes that kept his head locked into the long pole. His hands were still tied behind him, but Sengbe could see that they were freeing everyone's heads from the poles and some of the prisoners were being fed. He heard a clanging sound ringing out and could see

the white-faced men carrying long chains and hammers.   With
his hands still bound behind him, a metal band was put around
his neck. Tied to this band was a chain that led to another band
that was fastened to another man's neck. A different band and
chain was being tied to his foot. He tried to kick it away, but he
was held down. He was too tired and too hungry to fight.
And worse, his heart was sick.

After the chain was tied to his foot, Sengbe could see that
this chain was also tied to the foot of the other man. They
were truly linked together now. Sengbe was filled with rage,
but there was nothing he could do. His hands were still tied
and now his neck and his foot were also chained.

But he could smell food.

One by one, all the prisoners were being given water by
their captors. As Sengbe swallowed the last gulp, one of his
captors took out a knife and motioned to him to raise his
hands. Sengbe lifted his hands and the man cut the ropes that
had tied him for so many days. Sengbe grabbed at his wrists
and felt the deep valleys in his skin that had been cut by the
ropes. Then, he was handed a bowl of rice and fish to eat.

Sengbe knew not to eat too fast, but savored each bite as
he chewed. He remembered when he was a child, that once he
had not eaten for days and when he finally was given food he
ate it all at once and then promptly got sick. This time he ate
slowly, letting his tongue push each piece of food around his
mouth. But not too slowly, for soon it was time to walk again.

They walked for another day and began to smell something in the air – something that smelled like salt. It was the
great ocean.

∿ FIVE ∿

Sengbe knew about the ocean. He had heard stories from his grandparents about the men and women who were carried into its belly by giant boats and were never seen again. Many of the other men and women must have heard these same stories because, when the water came into view, Sengbe could hear the screams and cries coming up and down the line of all those who were chained together.

When they reached the water, they were all herded onto the big boats and thrown down below the decks. Not quite into the belly of the ocean, but surely into the belly of this big ship, Sengbe thought.

The space underneath the ship's deck was very small – so small that no one could stand up in it. Though he was unable to see anything from his spot under the deck of the ship, Sengbe and the other captives could feel when the boat began to leave the shore. They could hear the noise of the men who commanded the boat and they could hear the sound of footsteps on the deck above them. There was a collective moan from the captives as they realized they were being taken away from their homeland. They were leaving Africa.

"We have been stolen," Sengbe thought.

Chained like beasts and unable to move from their position, they sat in the suffocating heat of the ship's belly for weeks with only rice and fish to eat and water to drink. If they did not eat, they were flogged and whipped. Many of them threw up the food they were given and their waste was left to dry where it was. There was no privacy and no room for any of them to move about. The ship smelled of urine and sweat and the foulest odors that Sengbe could imagine.

Many prisoners got sick and died.

Sengbe could feel the bites of fleas and lice on his body and saw that rats walked freely among the captives in the darkness below the deck. These rats had more freedom than he had, Sengbe realized. They were now nothing more than animals, herded together, eating and defecating in front of everyone else.

One of the stolen men told the others stories at night. Not everyone could understand the man's Mende words, but Sengbe did.

"They were now slaves," the storyteller said. "Captured not by devils, but by men who were slave traders." They were being taken to an island very far away from their homes. An island called Cuba. There, they would be sold and taken as slaves to work cutting sugar cane.

Sengbe hoped the man was making these stories up but the storyteller said he had been to this island before and had escaped and hidden on a boat coming back until he was discovered.

"Usually when you escape, they cut off your foot as an example to everyone else," the man said. But he was lucky. The slaver who recaptured him was not so cruel. He was whipped, the storyteller explained, as he paused to show everyone the deep scars on his back.

Yes, he was lucky, the storyteller said. He still had both his feet.

⊰ SIX ⊱

The stolen men and women sailed like this for weeks. They were fed once a day, usually a bowl of beans or rice or corn mush and fish. Eventually, if the weather was good, they were brought on deck for an hour or two and allowed to stand in the sun, still chained to one another.

The slavers would use their whips, forcing them to walk the deck of the ship in giant circles. Sengbe did not mind the walk. His legs hurt from being cramped and he looked forward to the exercise and the stretching the walk provided. Sengbe liked being on deck because the air was so much better than the foul smells down below.

And up on deck, Sengbe could watch the sun. Each time he was brought above he used the sun as a guide and noticed which way the ship was sailing. If he was to ever return to his home, he would need to go in the opposite direction.

Sengbe's neck was sore and swollen from the iron collar rubbing up against his skin. Once a week, the chained men and women would be brought up on deck where a man from the ship would pour powder around the iron collars on their necks and legs. Then he would put an ointment on their wounds.

This must be medicine, Sengbe thought, but that made no sense to him. Why beat someone with a whip until his back burned and bled and then put medicine on it? But then, nothing made sense to him anymore.

Many of the stolen men and women died from their wounds. Some died from infections caused by their iron collars.

Some died from hunger. And some, Sengbe knew, died from broken hearts.

Sengbe thought about his family often. He tried to picture the faces of his children in his mind. He did not want to forget them and he was afraid he would lose the memory of his family and everyone else he knew.

After they had been sailing for many weeks, Sengbe and the others were on deck when they heard screams coming from the other side of the ship. Sengbe could not see what was happening, but he could hear the white-faced men yelling as they pushed everyone back into the cargo hold.

Later, Sengbe learned that two of the stolen men who were chained together had tried to jump into the water to drown themselves, but were caught by the big nets hanging alongside the ship. They would have gone into the belly of the ocean for certain, Sengbe thought, if they had not been caught by the nets.

After that, the stolen men and women were not allowed up on deck as often – and then only in smaller groups where they could be watched more carefully.

Did people try to throw themselves into the ocean often, Sengbe wondered? Why else would they hang nets like that?

∽ SEVEN ∾

From the bottom of the ship, Sengbe could only guess what was going on above, on deck. His neck stung and he hoped he would not get the sickness that was killing so many of the others.

One morning he heard the sound of feet running very fast on deck and could hear lots of shouting back and forth. The hatch to the cargo hold was thrown open and the stolen men and women were being ordered above. For the first time since the two men had tried to throw themselves into the sea, they were all being brought up together.

Once on deck, Sengbe could see that one of the men on the ship had a long pipe in his hands which he held up to his eye. He was looking off towards the horizon through this pipe and shouting at the men. He was clearly looking at something that Sengbe and the others could not see, no matter how hard they tried.

The slave traders seemed afraid of something – something that was visible only by this man with the long pipe. "Was it magic that gave him this sight?" Sengbe wondered. The other slavers gathered everyone on the deck, very close to the ship's edge, where, Sengbe could now see, all the nets had been taken away.

Before, they had been afraid to let them near the edge for fear that more would throw themselves into the water and drown, but now with the nets taken away – from what Sengbe could make out – they were getting ready to throw the captives into the sea. All of them.

The slavers were shouting to each other and some seemed to be arguing back and forth but Sengbe could not understand their words. As some of the slaves began to realize that they were about to be thrown into the water, they began moving away from the edge of the ship, screaming and pushing. Some were crying. Some were shrieking. Some were praying and Sengbe recognized some of the Mende words. These were prayers Sengbe knew.

The man with the long eye pipe fired a pistol into the air and the noise silenced everyone for a moment as he command-ed the others who looked at him for direction. They took out their whips and began beating the captives back away from the edge of the boat and back down into the cargo hold.

Whatever danger there was, Sengbe realized, it was over. But they never got another chance to go up on deck again after that.

Sengbe knew they must be near land by the smell in the air. The smell was still like salt, but with other smells mixed in. Sengbe thought he could smell smoke from a fire pit.

And then, sitting under the deck in the cargo hold, he thought he could hear birds overhead; birds that were flying home to their nests. Birds that were flying free.

⌣ EIGHT ⌣

Four nights later, the ship stopped. The stolen men and
women who were still alive were lowered into small boats and
rowed ashore in the dark night, still chained to each other.
Sengbe could see that many did not get off the boat.

Over half had died on the long voyage. The ones that had
reached land were then marched into the forest and locked
inside small huts that had been built for them.

The next morning, a man in a long white coat entered
Sengbe's hut and pointed at the chains that were around his
neck. Another man removed the chains.

The man in the long coat visited him later that day carrying a foul smelling cream that he put around Sengbe's neck and
over the open sores he had on his leg. Some of the slaves
fought this, but Sengbe realized that like the ointment they
were given on the ship, this was medicine.

After a few days in the huts, Sengbe realized that something had changed. There were no more beatings. They were
fed well and given plenty to drink.

After a week, a white-faced man approached Sengbe and
held his hand over Sengbe's heart. "Sin Kay," the man said
over and over again. "Jo Sef Sin Kay." The man said these
words over and over and motioned for Sengbe to say them.
These were funny sounding words to Sengbe. "Sin Kay," the
man repeated, "Jo Sef Sin Kay."

⌁ NINE ⌁

Sin Kay. Jo Sef Sin Kay. Was this a name? Was this the man's name? Sengbe did not understand this strange new language and tried to speak his Mende words but the man held up his hand in front of him and closed his eyes to signal that Sengbe stop. The man repeated the strange words one more time and then left.

Sengbe and the others were allowed to rest for another week. They were fed regularly and given oil to rub into their skin. Their wounds healed and they were able to get stronger. They were marched to a big village and then placed in a big pen with a dirt floor surrounded by a fence on all four sides. It was a stockade, Sengbe realized, like the ones they kept their animals in at home.

While in the stockade, men came by and looked at them all. They looked at their teeth and eyes and felt the muscles in their arms and legs. They looked at the women and the children, too. Sengbe saw one man pointing at him and then giving the man Sengbe knew only as Sin Kay some coins and papers. Was he being sold, Sengbe wondered?

◡ TEN ◡

Three days later, Sengbe and some of the other stolen men were taken out of the pen and moved to another location along with four small children. Some of these were men Sengbe recognized from his ship. Others, Sengbe thought, must have come from ships just like it.

That afternoon the stolen men were taken aboard another ship. It was smaller than the one that had brought them to this place. The children began screaming and pulling away when they realized they were being taken to another ship.

As they boarded the ship, Sengbe saw that some of the men had whips and they were laughing and talking together. One man had a long pipe and was smoking. The smell in his pipe reminded Sengbe of the smells at home when the old men smoked their pipes by the fires.

Sengbe yearned to be home. How had he ended up here? Were they all going to die on another long voyage?

There were not as many white-faced men on this ship as there had been on the bigger boat. But then Sengbe only counted fifty-three captives, far less than had set sail on the big ship from his home country. And Sengbe was happy to discover that many of these captives even spoke his language.

⌁ ELEVEN ⌁

On board, Sengbe saw the captain and his crew members. He also saw the man who had bought him, as well as another man who was buying stolen men at the market. This man was shouting out strange sounding words and pointing at the stolen men. He said the name Sin Kay and Sengbe looked around for the white man who called himself Sin Kay, but he was not there.

The man approached Sengbe and repeated the words "Sin Kay." Sengbe knew these words and nodded to the man. The man looked right at him as he said the words again. He pointed at Sengbe and repeated the words. He put his hand on Sengbe's chest and said the words once more.

This process was repeated with each passenger and Sengbe realized that the stories he had heard when he was a boy were true. Sengbe now knew that it was he – Sengbe Pieh – who was to be called Joseph Cinque.

These men were devils after all. They had taken away his life and they had taken away his name, too.

But why? Why would they want to steal his name and give him another? There was much to learn about these devils.

~ TWELVE ~

The new ship set sail with fifty-three slaves and a small crew to guard them. The slaves were kept down below, chained together. It would be a short voyage, the Captain of the ship thought.

Down below, the stolen men had a different plan. "I have been watching the sun," Sengbe told them in their Mende language. "I know the direction that will take us home. We can go back!"

He shared his plan with the others, thankful that most could understand his words and he could communicate his thoughts as the others nodded in agreement.

Sengbe thought of what the captured slave from the first boat had said. "If you run away, they usually cut off your foot." What would they do to him and the others if they were not successful? Running away was one thing, but taking the boat and killing some of the devils was something else, Sengbe knew. They would be killed, for sure, if they were captured.

But what did the stolen men have to lose? Could they live the rest of their lives like this, chained like animals? Sengbe knew he could not.

Sengbe showed the others a nail that he found on board. He used the nail to open the lock on his chain and then sprung another man from his chains. One by one, each captive was released as they worked quietly below the ship's deck.

The waves lapped against the ship as it sailed through the night. Sengbe and the others made their way to the deck.

There, they found a box of knives. Some grabbed sticks or anything that could be used as a weapon.

Sengbe took one of the knives he had found and walked quietly in the darkness. He saw the captain of the ship sleeping on the deck of the ship in the cool night air. Sengbe raised his knife and struck the captain as he slept. Other Mende men surrounded the captain and strangled him with their bare hands as the blood from Sengbe's knife poured onto the deck.

It was not a fair fight, Sengbe knew, but nothing that had happened to them since their capture had been fair and they were taking no chances.

There was confusion on the ship in the darkness. The stolen men were screaming now – happy screams, but filled with fear. Two of the white-faced sailors jumped overboard. Did they escape on one of the smaller boats tied to the ship or did they drown? In the confusion on board, no one knew for sure. Three of the stolen men had been killed in the fight to take the ship.

The two men who had bought the slaves in the market were taken prisoner and tied up with ropes that the stolen men had found on board. They were not chained by the neck or legs with iron bands like the stolen men had been – but now it was these slave traders who were no longer free.

Sengbe wanted to kill these men but some of the other Mende men persuaded him not to. These men could sail the ship back and take them home.

It was hard to see everything that was happening as the ship sailed on in the darkness, lit only by the stars and a few lanterns that moved and swayed with the ocean's pitch. But Sengbe knew they were in charge now

⌒ THIRTEEN ⌒

The stolen men were now in charge, but they could not control a ship like this. Sengbe and the other Mende men had been on smaller boats on the rivers in their own lands but none had ever sailed a vessel this big on an ocean that seemed to go on forever.

During the trip from his country, Sengbe knew the sun had always been on the same side of the ship. At dawn, he commanded that the two white men be untied and then motioned to them to sail the ship in the other direction, back to their home lands. As he pointed to the sun, he spoke excitedly. The white-faced men nodded their heads to signal that they understood what he wanted. They knew he wanted to go home and turned the ship in the direction that Sengbe had commanded.

They sailed for weeks. The two white-faced men smiled and talked quietly to each other whenever any of the stolen men approached and this made Sengbe uncomfortable. They were beginning to run out of food and water. This journey was long and the days were hot. Sengbe did not know just how smart these devils were. He did not know that every night, when the sun went down, the slave traders changed the direction of the ship, sailing away from the homes of the stolen men.

The journey lasted many weeks because they kept zig-zagging back and forth. First they would go east towards home during the day; then westward in the other direction at night.

Eventually they saw land, but the land was unfamiliar and Sengbe and the stolen men knew that they had been tricked.

❧ FOURTEEN ❧

What could they do? Some had died while they were at sea and others were sick. They were all hungry and had little water left, so Sengbe and a few of the Mende men took a rowboat to shore. They had found a box of gold coins on board and took some of the gold with them in case they found someone who could sail them back to their homeland.

But they did not find someone to sail them back home. Instead, the stolen men were taken prisoner again by more white-faced men with guns who were on a big boat that pulled up alongside of theirs. They were in a new land now. It was a strange land that Sengbe had never heard of before; a land called America.

And in America, it was unusual for black men with only a few clothes on their backs to have so much gold. It was unusual for black men who could not speak the language to wave their hands in the air and point at boats and shout loudly. And it was unusual to have a ship filled with slaves who could successfully fight back and gain control of the boat that brought them to these shores.

In America, this was news.

∴ FIFTEEN ∾

Sengbe and the other stolen men would be taken before judges who would decide what would happen to them. This was the same way things were decided back home, Sengbe thought. But back home, Sengbe could speak freely in a language that could be understood by his judges.

Here, he spoke words that no one understood. How could he tell the judges the story of his capture? How could he tell them of his life in another land – a life with his children and wife? Who would speak for him? Each of the stolen men had a story just like his but how could he tell it? Would anyone even listen?

Some of the people in this strange land knew that the stolen men needed someone to speak for them and there were many white-faced men who helped them – white-faced men who were not devils. They found an African man named James – a boy really – who lived in this new country and spoke its language. Like Sengbe, James had been captured in Mende country and then taken out of Africa by slave traders. But he was taken away from the slave traders and taught the strange English words of this new country. He also knew many of the Mende words and Sengbe and the others were happy to hear them when he spoke. This boy would help the stolen men who took part in the rebellion at sea by speaking their words. But it would take time.

Sengbe would soon discover many more things about this strange new country. He would find out that many people in this new land thought that he and the other stolen men should be set free. Others thought they should be returned to the slave traders who had purchased them as property because the slave owners had papers that showed the Mende men belonged to them and were from the island of Cuba. Some even wanted Sengbe and the stolen men to hang for the murder of the ship's captain.

∿ SIXTEEN ∿

The stolen men were put in a jail until the judges decided what to do with them; not chained together, but still not free.

While in jail, Sengbe learned many of the English words and began to piece together all that had happened to him. This new country had strange laws. Men could own slaves just as they could in his country, but Sengbe learned that this new country had rules that made it illegal to capture free people in Africa and bring them over and make them slaves here. But that was exactly what had been done to Sengbe and the other stolen men.

Sengbe learned that if a slave trader was caught trying to bring in new slaves, the penalty could be death. Maybe that was why they were ready to drown all the slaves in the sea, Sengbe thought. They must have seen a ship approaching and rather than risk being discovered, they were going to drown every last man, woman and child on board. It was a good thing the other ship had decided to turn around.

And that must have also been the reason they gave Sengbe a new name – a Spanish name. They were trying to prove that he had always been a slave on that island where the first ship had stopped, and owned by the slave traders. But Sengbe didn't speak English – or Spanish. Wasn't it clear that he and the others had come from Africa and that they were newly-captured slaves?

Sengbe knew that if these judges were fair, they would allow them all to go home.

But would these judges be fair? None of the men who brought them to this place were good people and to many people in this new land, they were nothing more than property – owned by the white men who had purchased them and then tricked them by sailing in the wrong direction.

Property! Sengbe thought. He was no man's property and would never be.

How could these strange men tell him what was fair?

⌐ SEVENTEEN ⌐

The stolen men went before the judges. Sengbe understood little of what the white men said but he knew that the Mende were all in trouble for the murder of the Captain. Sengbe had learned some words but he did not need them to understand that there was much disagreement and arguing in the council.

The white-faced men shouted words and pointed at Sengbe often. Sengbe recognized some of the words being spoken in the law council. He heard the words "slavery" many times and heard men say that laws had been broken. Which laws, Sengbe wondered? Were they talking about the slavery laws of this strange country or the murder of the captain? Other men spoke about fighting for freedom, fighting for justice, fighting for liberty. These were words that Sengbe had learned.

Then it was Sengbe's turn to talk. He used the words he had learned as he told his story, but mostly he spoke from his heart in his own language. He spoke about his capture and his desire to go back home. And as he spoke, he used more and more of the Mende words that came to him. He spoke about the conditions on the slave ship and he told the law council what had happened. As he spoke, the boy James spoke the words in English.

All the chiefs of the law council listened quietly and nodded, but Sengbe wondered if any of them really understood his heart.

⌐ EIGHTEEN ⌐

There would be other meetings of the Council. Sometimes the men who were helping Sengbe seemed very happy with what went on there. Sometimes they did not. There were many meetings and many councils and then it was announced that the case of the stolen men would be heard by a Great Council that would meet in another village far away. The stolen men would not even be there.

Other men would tell their story to the Great Law Council of judges who would gather to hear the story of their capture and decide their fate. One of the men who would help tell the stolen men's story was a Chief. This Chief – called President by the strange Americans – used to be the leader of the whole country, Sengbe was told. But now he was old and not the leader anymore. This chief would argue for the men before the Great Law Council and the Law Council would listen to what he had to say.

What kind of a country was this, Sengbe wondered? How could they decide his fate without hearing his words and listening to his story?

The Great Law Council would decide his fate based on words from other men – men who were not even on the ship. Men who were not taken from their families and chained together. Men who could only imagine what it was like to survive that kind of a voyage.

But this is how it worked here in this strange, new land and all Sengbe could do was wait.

~: NINETEEN :~

And then, it was over. The Great Law Council had made their decision. Sengbe and the other men were to be set free. The Council of Judges had decided that because they were stolen – captured illegally from their homeland – they were now free to return.

Many of the men and women who helped Sengbe and the other captives in their trial, now helped arrange for a ship to take them back to the Mende lands in Africa.

Finally, they would be able to return home.

~: TWENTY :~

Standing on the deck of yet another ship, Sengbe and thirty-four other free men were finally heading back home to their country – and to their families.

Some of the stolen men had died in the new country. But thirty-five were coming home. Not as cattle, yoked around the neck. Not as property chained together. But as free people. They could walk on the deck of this vessel when they wanted to. They were no longer chained together and beaten.

It had been three years since Sengbe had been stolen. Could he find his village again? Would he be able to find his wife alive? Would his children be well? They had been so young when he was taken. Would they even remember him?

He had many questions inside his mind as he watched the sun setting a bright orange color on the horizon. But he was on a ship that was finally carrying him home; carrying him back to a part of his life that had been taken from him so long ago.

And he was not afraid of what lay ahead.

⌐ ABOUT THIS BOOK ⌐

The story of Sengbe Pieh is a true one. I began writing this book in 1994, many years after first reading about his story. I was struck by so many elements in the story and surprised that I had never heard anything about this event in our nation's history before.

I worked on this book for many years, losing my enthusiasm for it when I read that a film was going to be made about it – and that there would be many books for children coming out that would tie in with the movie. The story would be told!

Many years after the movie *Amistad* came out, I was giving a school presentation in Virginia and was asked if I had ever written a chapter book for children. Remembering my story, I dug it out after years of having it filed away and began to work on it again.

I am happy to say that there is now much information about Sengbe Pieh – also known by his "given" name of Joseph Cinque – and the Amistad ship rebellion. There are wonderful web sites devoted to telling this story and there are many books on the Amistad rebellion but none have been written from Sengbe's point of view.

I think his story needs to be told and it's a good place for early readers to discover this fascinating historical event.

-Barry Louis Polisar

Also by Barry Louis Polisar:

Books
Peculiar Zoo

Insect Soup

A Little Less Noise

Don't Do That

Snakes and The Boy Who Was Afraid of Them

The Snake Who Was Afraid of People

The Trouble With Ben

The Haunted House Party

Dinosaurs I Have Known

Noises from Under the Rug

CD Recordings
Old Enough To Know Better

A Little Different

Old Dogs, New Tricks

Teacher's Favorites

Family Trip

Naughty Songs for Boys & Girls

Juggling Babies

Family Concert

Off-Color Songs for Kids

Stanley Stole My Shoelace and Rubbed It in His Armpit

Songs for Well-Behaved Children

Captured Live and in the Act

My Brother Thinks He's a Banana

I Eat Kids and Other Songs for Rebellious Children